I0759482

POCKETBOOKS
by BroadStreet

100 Bible Promises for Girls

BroadStreet KIDS

BroadStreet Kids
Savage, Minnesota, USA
BroadStreet Kids is an imprint of BroadStreet Publishing Group, LLC.
Broadstreetpublishing.com

100 Bible Promises for Girls

9781424571628
9781424571635 eBook

Entries composed by Jeanna Harder.

Typesetting and design by Garborg Design Works | garborgdesign.com
Editorial services by Michelle Winger | literallyprecise.com

Printed in China.

26 27 28 29 30 31 32 7 6 5 4 3 2 1

God says...

Introduction

This book is filled with God's words for you. Short, powerful verses from the Bible will remind you how much God loves you and is always with you—no matter what.

Perfect for bedtime, quiet time, or anytime you need to feel God's love, this small book is great to keep close wherever you go.

You are beautiful, you are brave, and you are loved by God. His promises are forever!

1

God Is Your Strong Tower

The Lord is like a strong tower.
Those who do what is right
can run to him for safety.

PROVERBS 18:10 ICB

When you feel afraid, you can pray to God and ask him to protect you. He is like a big, strong tower. He will keep you safe.

Thank you, God, for being my strong tower where I can run for safety.

2

God Makes Things New

"Look at the new thing I am going to do. It is already happening. Don't you see it?"

ISAIAH 43:19 ICB

When you feel sad or disappointed, talk to God about your feelings. He is able to make things new. He can make something good out of a sad situation.

Dear God, thank you for making things better.

3

God Gives You Strength

I can do all things through Christ because he gives me strength.

PHILIPPIANS 4:13 ICB

Jesus is full of strength and power. He loves to give you what you need. Go ahead and ask him right now to make you stronger to do something.

Dear Jesus, please give me strength to make good choices.

4

God Gives You Wisdom

If any of you needs wisdom, you should ask God for it. He will give it to you. God gives freely to everyone and doesn't find fault.

JAMES 1:5 NIRV

When you don't know what to do, ask God for help. He always knows what's best. Ask God for wisdom and he will give it to you.

Thank you, God, for giving me wisdom when I don't know what to do.

God is with you.

5

God Makes You Healthy

Don't depend on your own wisdom.
Respect the Lord and refuse to do wrong.
Then your body will be healthy.

PROVERBS 3:7-8 ICB

Try your best to do what's right and stop doing what is wrong. Show God that you respect him, and he will help keep your mind and body healthy.

Dear God, help me to be healthy by making good choices.

6

God Is Greater

You belong to God. So you have defeated them because God's Spirit, who is in you, is greater than the devil, who is in the world.

1 JOHN 4:4 ICB

It is a huge relief to know that no matter what, God is greater than all of your problems. He has the power to save you, and he loves you so much. With God on your side, you can beat anything that stands in your way!

Thank you, God, for being greater than anything in the world.

7

God Is Your Shield

Surely, LORD, you bless those
who do what is right.
Like a shield, your loving care
keeps them safe.

PSALM 5:12 NIRV

God is so loving and caring. He blesses those who do what is right and keeps them safe. He is like a huge shield protecting you from evil.

Thank you, God, for taking care of me and protecting me. Help me do what is right.

8

God Is Your Rock

My God is my rock.
I can run to him for safety.
He is my shield and my saving strength.

2 SAMUEL 22:3 ICB

God is like a rock. He doesn't change, and he is strong. Run to him when you need his help. He will keep you safe.

Dear God, keep me safe and shield me from temptation.

God listens to you.

9

God Gives You a Way Out

You are tempted in the same way all other human beings are. God is faithful. He will not let you be tempted any more than you can take. But when you are tempted, God will give you a way out.

1 CORINTHIANS 10:13 NIRV

Everyone is tempted to do what is wrong, but God is so good. He promises not to let you be tempted more than you can handle. He will always give you a way out.

Dear God, thank you for showing me how to get away from temptation.

10

God Leads You

The true children of God are those who let God's Spirit lead them.

ROMANS 8:14 ICB

As a child of God, you have his Spirit inside you. He is your helper. He will lead and guide you. Listen to his soft voice.

Dear God, help me to listen to your Holy Spirit leading me.

11

God Helps You

"I will ask the Father. And he will give you another friend to help you and to be with you forever."

JOHN 14:16 NIRV

Jesus asked, and God gave the Holy Spirit to help you. The Holy Spirit is like a friend who is always with you wherever you go.

Thank you, God, for giving me the Holy Spirit as my friend and helper.

12

God Makes You Strong

You have become weak. So make yourselves strong again. Keep on the right path so the weak will not stumble but rather be strengthened.

HEBREWS 12:12-13 ICB

Some days are hard, and you might feel weak. Keep following Jesus. Stay on the right path, and he will make you strong.

Dear Jesus, help me when I am weak. I want to get stronger as I follow you.

God gives you peace.

13

God Is With You

*"Don't worry, because I am with you.
Don't be afraid, because I am your God.
I will make you strong and will help you."*

ISAIAH 41:10 ICB

Worries can pop into your head and make you feel afraid. God says not to worry because he promises to always be with you and help you.

*Dear God, I give you my worries.
Thank you for being with me.*

14

God Takes Away Your Worry

Don't worry about anything. No matter what happens, tell God about everything. Ask and pray, and give thanks to him. Then God's peace will watch over your hearts and your minds.

PHILIPPIANS 4:6-7 NIRV

When you pray, thank God and ask him to take care of your worries. He will! And even better, he will fill your heart and mind with peace instead.

Thank you, God, for taking care of my worries and replacing them with peace.

15

God Gives You Peace

May the Lord who gives peace give you peace at all times and in every way. May the Lord be with all of you.

2 THESSALONIANS 3:16 NIRV

Even when you are in the middle of a scary situation, God can give you peace. He is always with you, and he is always able to do what seems impossible.

Dear God, give me peace in my heart when I am nervous or afraid.

16

God Is Trustworthy

When I am afraid,
I will trust you.
I praise God for his word.
I trust God. So I am not afraid.

PSALM 56:3-4 ICB

You can trust God. His Word, the Bible, is full of examples of people who were afraid. But God proved he could be trusted. Read about Noah or Moses or Daniel!

Thank you, God, for all the examples in the Bible about trusting you.

God wants you to be with him.

17

God Gives You Power

God gave us his Spirit. And the Spirit doesn't make us weak and fearful. Instead, the Spirit gives us power and love. He helps us control ourselves.

2 TIMOTHY 1:7 NIRV

The Holy Spirit is like a superhero! He gives you power. When you need help controlling your temper, ask the Holy Spirit to give you power.

Thank you, God, for giving me power from the Holy Spirit.

18

God Helps You When You Are Angry

Always be willing to listen and slow to speak. Do not become angry easily. Anger will not help you live a good life as God wants.

JAMES 1:19-2 ICB

How do you feel when you are angry? You probably don't feel good. God wants you to live a good life. Don't let anger get in the way of you having a good day.

Dear, God, help me control my anger and live a good life.

19

God Gives You Happiness

Examine and see how good the Lord is.
Happy is the person who trusts the Lord.

Psalm 34:8 ICB

Fear and worry steal your joy. Trusting God to take care of you changes those worries into happiness. Think about how good God has been to you.

Dear God, thank you for being good to me and filling me with happiness.

20

God Still Does Miracles

"With God, all things are possible."

MATTHEW 19:26 NIRV

Miracles are when God uses his amazing power to do impossible things. Can you think of some miracles you know about and praise God for them right now? God makes all things possible.

Dear God, I praise you for the miracles you have done.

God has a place
for you.

21

God Shows You Mercy

"I am the Lord. The Lord is a God who shows mercy and is kind."

EXODUS 34:6 ICB

It is easy to get mad when someone does something mean to you, but God wants you to do the opposite. He wants you to show mercy. He will show you mercy when you do the same for others.

Dear God, help me show mercy to others.

22

God Forgives Every Time

If we confess our sins, he will forgive our sins. He will forgive every wrong thing we have done.

1 JOHN 1:9 NIRV

Have you ever done something really bad? Don't worry. God promises that he will forgive you every time you are sorry and confess the wrong thing you have done.

Thank you, God, that no matter what I have done, you will always forgive me.

23

God Is the One Who Saves

LORD, you are the one who saves.
May your blessing be on your people.

PSALM 3:8 NIRV

God is the only one who has the power to save you from sin. He is ready and waiting for you receive his gift of salvation. You can do it right now.

Dear God, please forgive me for my sin.

24

God Gives You Eternal Life

"God loved the world so much that he gave his only Son. God gave his Son so that whoever believes in him may not be lost, but have eternal life."

JOHN 3:16 ICB

Because of God's deep love, he sent his only Son, Jesus, to die for you. This means that you can be forgiven of your sins and live forever with him in heaven.

Thank you, Jesus, for dying for my sins so I can have eternal life.

God makes you strong.

25

God Has a Place for You

"There are many rooms in my Father's house. I would not tell you this if it were not true. I am going there to prepare a place for you."

JOHN 14:2 NIRV

After Jesus rose from the dead, he went back to heaven and prepared a place for you. There's a room ready for you in God's house. Isn't that exciting?

Dear Jesus, thank you for preparing a room for me in God's house.

26

God Makes You Glad

You always gave him blessings.
You made him glad because you
were with him.

PSALM 21:6 ICB

God loves to bless his children. Don't you love it when you get gifts? Doesn't it make your heart glad? Having God as your Father is the very best gift of all.

Thank you, God, for your gifts that make me glad.

27

God Teaches You

"He will teach you all things. He will remind you of everything I have said to you."

JOHN 14:26 NIRV

The goal of learning is to remember what you have been taught. When God teaches you something, let it go deep into your heart. Then ask him to remind you when you forget!

Dear God, help me remember what I have learned from you.

28

God Gives You Good Sense

Pay attention to my wisdom.
Listen carefully to my wise sayings.
Then you will continue to have good sense.

PROVERBS 5:1-2 ICB

Wisdom is so good to have. It helps you make decisions and know what to do. Good sense from God is something you need.

Dear God, please give me good sense to know what to do.

God keeps you safe.

29

God Gives You a Great Example

Do what you have learned or received or heard from me. Follow my example. The God who gives peace will be with you.

PHILIPPIANS 4:9 NIRV

When you don't know what to do, think about what Jesus would do. If you follow Jesus, he will always be with you, and he will show you what to do.

Thank you, Jesus, for your great example.

30

God Helps You Avoid Traps

The LORD will be at your side.
He will keep your feet
from being caught in a trap.

PROVERBS 3:26 NIRV

Temptation is a way the devil tries to trap you into making wrong choices. God can show you the devil's traps and help you stay away from them.

Thank you, God, for helping me stay away from the devil's traps.

31

God Lights the Way

Your word is like a lamp that
shows me the way.
It is like a light that guides me.

PSALM 119:105 NIRV

The Bible is full of God's words that teach, warn, and guide you. It's like a book of instructions that lights up the path for the best way to live. He can help you follow his path.

Thank you, God, for lighting the way for me.

32

God Decides Your Steps

In their hearts human beings
plan their lives.
But the LORD decides where their
steps will take them.

PROVERBS 16:9 NIRV

It is good to have dreams and to make plans. God has amazing plans for you too. Ask him what steps he has decided for you.

Dear God, what do you have planned for me today?

God is your helper.

33

God Gives You Freedom

You were chosen to be free. But don't use your freedom as an excuse to live under the power of sin. Instead, serve one another in love.

GALATIANS 5:13 NIRV

God is so kind. He gives you the freedom to choose whether to do good or to sin. You can choose to love God and serve others or to be selfish and only serve yourself. Make the best choice today!

Dear God, help me use my freedom to make good choices.

34

God Rewards Hard Work

Work as serving the Lord and not as serving people. You know that the Lord will give each person a reward.

EPHESIANS 6:7-8 NIRV

It is good to know that God will give you a reward for your hard work. Serve God and serve the people around you. Your reward is coming.

Thank you, God, for giving me a reward for my work.

35

God Is Generous

"Give, and you will receive. You will be given much. It will be poured into your hands—more than you can hold. You will be given so much that it will spill into your lap. The way you give to others is the way God will give to you."

LUKE 6:38 ICB

God is very generous. He will give more to you than you can ever give to others. He will give you so much that it will overflow into your lap!

Thank you, God, for being so generous to me when I give to others.

36

God Gives Mercy and Grace

Let us, then, feel free to come before God's throne. Here there is grace. And we can receive mercy and grace to help us when we need it.

HEBREWS 4:16 ICB

You can always go to God when you need him. He will show you grace when you come to him with a heart that says, "I'm sorry." You don't need to be afraid to confess your sin and ask for help.

Dear God, help me come to you often. Thank you that you want me to be with you.

God will never reject you.

37

God Blesses You When You Don't Give Up

People who don't give up are blessed. You have heard that Job was patient. And you have seen what the Lord finally did for him.

JAMES 5:11 NIRV

Don't give up when things are hard. A man in the Bible named Job went through many difficult things. But he did not give up on God. Try to keep doing your best. God sees your hard work, and he will bless you for it.

Dear God, help me not to give up when things are hard.

38

God Knows When You Are Hurting

He doesn't forget the cries of those who are hurting.

PSALM 9:12 NIRV

Your parents probably hear you crying when you get hurt. God does too. He cares about you. If no one else notices your sadness, God does. He will always be with you.

Thank you, God, for caring about me when I am hurt.

39

God Watches Over You

The Lord watches over the lives of the innocent.

Psalm 37:18 ICB

God watches over you. When you feel afraid or you are worried, remember that the God of the whole universe always sees you.

Thank you, God, for watching over me.

40

God Protects You

Love the Lord, all you who belong to him. The Lord protects those who truly believe.

PSALM 31:23 ICB

One of the jobs of a mother and father is to protect their children. God the Father does the same thing. He protects those who belong to him. You are his daughter, so you can be sure that he protects you.

Thank you, God, for protecting me.

God teaches you.

41

God Calls You His Child

See what amazing love the Father has given us! Because of it, we are called children of God. And that's what we really are!

1 JOHN 3:1 NIRV

Can you imagine loving someone so much that you make them part of your family? That's how God feels about you. You are loved by God so much that he calls you his precious daughter.

Thank you, God, for loving me so much that you call me your child.

42

God Makes You New

If anyone belongs to Christ, then he is made new. The old things have gone; everything is made new!

2 CORINTHIANS 5:17 ICB

Being made new means all your sin is washed away. You stop doing the bad things you know are wrong, and you choose what is good instead. It's like taking a bath and washing away all the dirt.

Dear God, please wash me clean and make me new.

43

God Helps You to Be Good

God is working in you to help you want to do what pleases him. Then he gives you the power to do it.

PHILIPPIANS 2:13 ICB

God doesn't expect you to be perfect. He knows you need help making good choices, and he is so proud of you when you do. He is ready to help when you need it.

Dear God, I want to do what pleases you. Help me.

44

God's Love for You Never Ends

"The mountains may disappear,
and the hills may come to an end.
But my love will never disappear."

ISAIAH 54:10 ICB

No matter what you do or how big of a mistake you make, God will never stop loving you. You are so to him. He will never run out of love for you.

Dear God, thank you for loving me forever.

God is patient
with you.

45

God Makes Things Go Well

"I'm giving you his rules and commands today. Obey them. Then things will go well with you and your children after you."

DEUTERONOMY 4:40 NIRV

God promises that if you obey him, then he will make things go well for you. Things won't always be easy, but God will work it all out for you in the end if you obey him.

Thank you, God, for making things go well for me.

46

God Gives You What You Need

God supplies seed for the person who plants. He supplies bread for food. God will also supply and increase the amount of your seed. He will increase the results of your good works.

2 CORINTHIANS 9:10 ICB

You might not be a farmer, but the promise in this verse is for you. God will give you what you need. You will not go hungry, and your work will be rewarded.

Thank you, God, for giving me what I need.

47

God Calls You Friend

"I call you friends because I have made known to you everything I heard from my Father."

JOHN 15:15 ICB

Friends are special people in your life. Jesus had friends when he lived on the earth. Now he calls you his friend. What an amazing friend he is!

Thank you, Jesus, for calling me your friend.

48

God Has Riches in Heaven for You

"Store up riches in heaven that will never be used up. There, no thief can come near it. There, no moth can destroy it. Your heart will be where your riches are."

LUKE 12:33-34 NIRV

Isn't it fun to know there will be riches in heaven? Nothing will get ruined or broken in heaven, and nothing can be taken away or stolen from you there. Build riches in heaven by obeying God while you are here.

Thank you, God, for the riches you have waiting for me in heaven.

God is on
your side.

49

God Is Always Available

Be my place of safety
where I can always come.

PSALM 71:3 ICB

No matter where you are or what time it is, God is always available to you. He is never too busy. You can go to him any time and tell him anything you want.

Thank you, God, for always being available.

50

God Proves He Is Real

The heavens tell the glory of God.
And the skies announce
what his hands have made.

PSALM 19:1 ICB

Think of all the amazing things God created like rainbows, seasons, giant whales, and colorful birds. Think of how everything works together. Nature proves there is a God.

Dear God, I know you are real by looking at nature.

51

God Has Special Work for You

God has made us what we are. In Christ Jesus, God made us new people so that we would do good works. God had planned in advance those good works for us. He had planned for us to live our lives doing them.

EPHESIANS 2:10 ICB

God has special work for you. There are things you need to learn to be able to do that work. Ask him how you can get started!

Dear God, please show me the good works you have for me to do.

52

God Wants You

God decided to make us his own children through Jesus Christ. That was what he wanted and what pleased him.

EPHESIANS 1:5 ICB

You are wanted by God. You are his favorite creation. You make him so happy just by being the wonderful girl he created you to be.

Thank you, God, for wanting me.

God knows how you feel.

53

God Makes You Secure

Good things will come to those
who are fair in everything they do.
Those who do what is right
will always be secure.

PSALM 112:5-6 NIRV

God sees everything you do. That shouldn't make you afraid. It means you are secure. God is pleased when you do what's right, and he is fair. Choose good things today!

Thank you, God, for noticing when I do what is right.

54

God Gives You Role Models

Brothers and sisters, join together in following my example. You have us as a model. So pay close attention to those who live as we do.

PHILIPPIANS 3:17 NIRV

God is so smart. He knew you would need help following Jesus, so he gave you role models to teach you and show you how to live the right way.

Thank you, God, for giving me role models to teach me about you.

55

God Gives You Family

God said, "It is not good for the man to be alone. I will make a helper who is just right for him."

GENESIS 2:18 NIRV

Families are very special. Who are the people in your family that help you the most? Who are the ones you enjoy being around? Who can you show love to in your family today?

Thank you, God, for my family.

56

God Gives Different Gifts

We all have gifts. They differ according to the grace God has given to each of us.

ROMANS 12:6 NIRV

God gives each person special gifts. Not everyone has the same. God gives you the perfect gift that will help you do the good work he has planned for you. Don't compare yourself to anyone else. Use your perfect gift!

Thank you, God, for giving me the perfect gift to do your work.

God sees you.

57

God Will Keep You Going

Turn your worries over to the LORD.
He will keep you going.
He will never let godly people be shaken.

PSALM 55:22 NIRV

What do you worry about? Give those worries to God. You don't want to have worries swirling around in your head day and night. Trust God to take care of you and keep you going.

Dear God, take my worries and keep me going.

58

God's Love Is the Best

Your love is better than life.
I will praise you.

PSALM 63:3 ICB

No one will love you as much as God loves you. His love is the best love you will ever feel. It's better than chocolate cake or puppies or Prince Charming. Praise God for his love.

Dear God, your love is the best in the whole world. Thank you.

59

God Gives You Confidence

We can feel sure and say,
"I will not be afraid because
the Lord is my helper.
People can't do anything to me."

HEBREWS 13:6 ICB

It is natural to feel afraid or uncomfortable at times. Maybe you don't like being in front of a crowd, or you are afraid to stand up to a bully. Pray and ask God to give you confidence. He will do it!

Dear God, when I am afraid or uncomfortable, please give me confidence.

60

God Knows Everything

"Everything that is hidden will become clear. Every secret thing will be made known."

LUKE 8:17 ICB

There is no secret that God does not know. Nothing is hidden from him. The truth will eventually come out. Don't try to lie or hide anything from God. He knows, and he understands.

Dear God, remind me that there is no need to hide anything from you.

God's love
never ends.

61

God Gives You Victory

Everyone who is a child of God has won the battle over the world. Our faith has won the battle for us.

1 JOHN 5:4 NIRV

When you fight against the evil in the world, God will help you win. You are a child of God, a princess of the true King. You are on the winning team.

Thank you, God, for giving me victory over the evil in the world.

62

God Makes You Innocent

Do everything without complaining or arguing. Then you will be innocent and without anything wrong in you. You will be God's children without fault.

PHILIPPIANS 2:14-15 ICB

Do you argue with your brother or sister too often? Do you complain a lot to your parents? The Bible says not to complain or argue, so try your best not to do those things. You can ask God to help you.

Dear God, help me not to complain or argue.

63

God Hears Your Prayers

The LORD is far away from
those who do wrong.
But he hears the prayers of
those who do right.

PROVERBS 15:29 NIRV

God hears your prayers. He loves it when you talk to him and share your thoughts and concerns. Your prayers are important. They matter to God. You matter to God. He loves you very much.

Thank you, God, for hearing my prayers.

64

God Will Satisfy You

Satisfy us with your faithful love
every morning.
Then we can sing for joy and be glad
all our days.

PSALM 90:14 NIRV

God knows what you need, and he knows what you love. He is a good father who loves to bring you joy and make your heart glad. Ask him to show you more of his love today!

Thank you, God, for satisfying me with your love every day.

God won't give up on you.

65

God Will Not Leave You

God does not leave us. We are hurt sometimes, but we are not destroyed.

2 CORINTHIANS 4:9 ICB

Do you ever feel lonely? God will never leave you. When your feelings get hurt by someone, God is there. When you feel left out, God is there. Talk to God about your feelings. He is always listening.

Dear Jesus, I am never alone because you are always with me.

66

God Takes Away Shame

The Lord God helps me.
So I will not be ashamed.

ISAIAH 50:7 ICB

It is normal to feel embarrassed or to regret something you wish you hadn't done. God can help you make a better choice next time. He doesn't shame you for your mistakes. He gives you grace when you ask.

Thank you, God for helping me and not shaming me.

67

God Has a Prize for You

We must not become tired of doing good. We will receive our harvest of eternal life at the right time. We must not give up!

GALATIANS 6:9 ICB

Don't give up! There will be times when you just don't feel like doing the right thing. You might be tired or frustrated. Keep trying. God will help you. He has a prize for you in heaven!

Dear God, help me not to give up on doing good things.

68

God Is Patient

The Lord is not slow in doing what he promised—the way some people understand slowness. But God is being patient with you.

2 PETER 3:9 ICB

God isn't in a rush, and he isn't slow. He will do what he has promised to do. He patiently waits for you to make your choice. He wants you to come to him.

Thank you, God, for being patient with me.

God gives you what you need.

69

God Wants to Forgive You

He doesn't become angry quickly.
He has great love.
He would rather forgive than punish.

JOEL 2:13 ICB

God is loving, kind, full of mercy, and slow to get angry. He wants to forgive you when you make a bad choice. Don't wait. Don't hide. Don't be afraid. Go right to God for forgiveness.

Dear God, thank you for forgiving me when I make bad choices.

70

God Is Kind

Let them give thanks to the LORD
for his faithful love.
Let them give thanks for the wonderful
things he does for people.

PSALM 107:8 NIRV

What are some of the wonderful things God has done for you and your family? Thank him in your own words. He loves it when you thank him for his kindness.

Thank you, God, for all the ways you show kindness to me.

71

God Is Gentle

"Accept my work and learn from me.
I am gentle and humble in spirit."

MATTHEW 11:2 NIRV

Would you rather have a teacher who is strict and mean, or one who is gentle, kind, and cheers you on? God is a gentle teacher. He doesn't get mad if you make a mistake. He encourages you to do your best.

Thank you, God, for being a gentle teacher.

72

God Wants You to Let Him In

"Here I am! I stand at the door and knock. If anyone hears my voice and opens the door, I will come in. I will eat with that person, and they will eat with me."

REVELATION 3:20 NIRV

God loves spending time with you, but he waits to be invited. He doesn't bang on the door of your heart like the Big Bad Wolf. He wants you to let him in but he won't force his way in. He is patient and gentle.

Thank you, God, for being loving, patient and gentle with me.

God is real.

73

God Made You a Special Gift

Children are a gift from the Lord.
Babies are a reward.

PSALM 127:3 ICB

Children are special to God, and he chose to give you as a gift to your parents. Remember that when the devil tries to trick you into thinking you aren't loved. You are a very special gift!

Dear God, please help me to remember that I am a gift from you.

74

God Gives Peaceful Sleep

I go to bed and sleep in peace.
Lord, only you keep me safe.

PSALM 4:8 ICB

How do you get ready for bed? Do you take a bath or shower? Do you read a book or a Bible story? Whatever you do, make time to pray and ask God for his peace to help you sleep.

Thank you, God, for helping me sleep in peace.

75

God Knows Your Needs

"Your Father knows that you need them. The thing you should seek is God's kingdom. Then all the other things you need will be given to you."

LUKE 12:30-32 ICB

Sometimes you need to speak up and ask people for what you want, but God already knows. Don't worry about the things you need. God knows, and he will provide.

Thank you, God, that you know what I need.

76

God Is Faithful

*Know that the Lord your God is God.
He is the faithful God. He will keep his
agreement of love for a thousand lifetimes.
He does this for people who love him and
obey his commands.*

DEUTERONOMY 7:9 ICB

When God makes a promise, he always keeps it. That is called faithfulness. Keeping a promise is doing what you say you're going to do. God will be faithful to do everything he said he will do.

Thank you, God, for being faithful and keeping your promises.

God made you special.

77

God Heals You

The LORD *will take care of them*
when they are lying sick in bed.
He will make them well again.

PSALM 41:3 NIRV

Have you been sick lately? Maybe a tummy ache, cold, cough, or fever? It doesn't feel good to be sick. You have to rest and take care of your body. Ask God to heal you because he can!

Thank you, God, for making me well when I am sick.

78

God Is Your Safe Place

Trust in him at all times, you people.
Tell him all your troubles.
God is our place of safety.

PSALM 62:8 NIRV

Tell God about your worries and troubles. You can trust him to always take care of you. He is a safe place to be honest. He is powerful enough to help you.

Dear God, thank you for being my safe place. I will trust you with my worries.

79

God Gives the Gift of Truth

You have the gift that the Holy One gave you. So you all know the truth.

1 JOHN 2:20 ICB

The Holy Spirit is God's gift for you. He tells your heart the truth about what's right and wrong. Listen to the Holy Spirit directing you.

Thank you, God, for giving me the Holy Spirit so I will know what is right and true.

80

God Is Your Savior

This is why we work and struggle. We hope in the living God. He is the Savior of all people. And in a very special way, he is the Savior of all who believe in him.

1 TIMOTHY 4:10 ICB

Somedays are a struggle, but you have hope. With God as your Savior, you have a wonderful future ahead of you. Choose to be hopeful even when things are hard.

Thank you, God, for saving me and giving me hope for a good future.

81

God Blesses You

The land produces its crops.
God, our God, blesses us.
May God continue to bless us.

PSALM 67:6-7 NIRV

Think of some things that God has blessed you with. Do you have grandparents you really love? Do you have pets? Do you have a favorite toy or a fun friend? God loves to bless you with good things.

Thank you, God, for all of the blessings you have given me.

82

God Gives You Armor

Put on all of God's armor. Evil days will come. But you will be able to stand up to anything.

EPHESIANS 6:13 NIRV

Armor is important. It protects you and gives you strength. The devil tries to defeat you with his evil plans, but you can fight back with God's armor helping you.

Thank you, God, for your armor that helps me fight.

God has a purpose for you.

83

God Will Defend You

"Don't be afraid! Stand still and see the LORD save you today."

EXODUS 14:13 ICB

The Bible is full of examples of God fighting for his people and defending them from evil. He will defend you too. Don't be afraid. Stay calm and let him save you.

Dear God, help me to be calm and remember that you will defend me.

84

God Will Comfort You

*"As a mother comforts her child,
I will comfort you."*

ISAIAH 66:13 NIRV

Children need to be comforted when they are hurt or afraid. Mothers do a great job of that. God is even better than a mother at comforting. Tell him what's wrong and ask him to comfort you.

Thank you, God, for comforting me when I am hurt and afraid.

85

God Sees Your Heart

"The LORD does not look at the things people look at. People look at the outside of a person. But the LORD looks at what is in the heart."

1 SAMUEL 16:7 NIRV

People can only see what you look like on the outside, but God can see right into your heart. He created you in a very special way for a very special reason. He loves who you are.

Thank you, God, for knowing who I really am.

86

God Fights for You

"The LORD your God is going with you. He'll fight for you. He'll help you win the battle over your enemies."

DEUTERONOMY 20:4 NIRV

What do you fight about? Do you fight with your brother, sister, or friend to get what you want? Do you fight against the devil to not make bad choices? God can help you with that! He fights for you.

Thank you, God, for fighting against evil and helping me win.

87

God Rewards Respect

A woman who respects the LORD
should be praised.
Give her the reward she has earned.

PROVERBS 31:30-31 NIRV

God notices how you behave. He is pleased when you respect him. You show this when you work hard and help others. He is so proud of you when you make good choices.

Dear God, I want to make you proud of me. Help me to always respect you.

88

God Honors Your Pain

"Blessed are you when people make fun of you and hurt you because of me."

MATTHEW 5:11 NIRV

Sometimes people are mean, and they make fun of those who believe in God. God will bless you when people cause you pain because you love and follow him.

Thank you, God, for blessing me when people make fun of me for following you.

God rewards hard work.

God Gives You Success

Remember the Lord in everything you do.
And he will give you success.

PROVERBS 3:6 ICB

When you obey God, he promises to give you success. Success is when things work out well for you. When you think about God, and you do what he wants you to do, he will work things out for you.

Thank you, God, for giving me success.

90

God Answers Prayers

*You answer us in amazing ways,
God our Savior.*

Psalm 65:5 ICB

God answers prayers. He might say yes to what you want, or he might say no. He might even say not yet, so you will have to wait. It may not always be the answer you want, but he will answer. And it will be the best thing for you.

Thank you, God, for answering my prayers.

91

God Has a Good Future for You

"I have good plans for you. I don't plan to hurt you. I plan to give you hope and a good future."

JEREMIAH 29:11 ICB

What do you want to be when you grow up? What are you good at? That may be part of God's good plans for you. Ask him what kind of future he has for you.

Thank you, God, for planning a good future for me.

92

God Makes a Way for You

There is only one way that people can reach God. That way is through Jesus Christ, who is also a man. Jesus gave himself to pay for the sins of all people.

1 TIMOTHY 2:5-6 ICB

There is only one way to get to God, and that is through Jesus. Sin separates you from God, but Jesus died on the cross to take away your sin. God made a way for you to come back to him through Jesus.

Thank you, God, for making a way for me to reach you.

93

God Made You Wonderful

How you made me is
amazing and wonderful.
I praise you for that.

PSALM 139:14 NIRV

Like snowflakes, everyone is different. No two people are the same. God is so creative! He made you wonderfully different than everyone else. Isn't that amazing?

Thank you, God, for the amazing and wonderful way you made me.

94

God Accepts Everyone

"God treats everyone the same," he said. "He accepts people from every nation. He accepts anyone who has respect for him and does what is right."

ACTS 10:34-35 NIRV

God doesn't only like certain people. He accepts everyone. He loves each person he creates no matter what they look like. He wants you to love and respect him and try your best to do the same for others.

Thank you, God, for accepting me and everyone else.

God is kind.

95

God Cares about You

"Not even one of the little birds can die without your Father's knowing it. God even knows how many hairs are on your head. So don't be afraid. You are worth much more than many birds."

MATTHEW 10:29-31 ICB

God cares about all of his creation. He knows what happens to each creature. But do you know who he cares about the most? You! You are worth so much to God.

Dear God, thank you for caring about me.

96

God Will Give You Life

"Honor your father and mother. Then you will live a long time in the land."

EXODUS 20:12 ICB

When you choose to do what your parents tell you to do, you are honoring them. When you say good things about them instead of bad things, that is also honoring them. God wants you to honor your parents. And when you do, he will give you life!

Dear God, help me to honor my mom and dad.

97

God Says You Are Precious

"Let the little children come to me. Don't keep them away. The kingdom of heaven belongs to people like them."

MATTHEW 19:14 NIRV

The disciples thought Jesus was too busy, too tired to be bothered by the parents who brought their children to him. But Jesus didn't feel like that at all! He loves children. You are precious to him.

Thank you, God, for loving children like me.

98

God Is Good

The LORD is good to all.
He shows deep concern
for everything he has made.

PSALM 145:9 NIRV

God is so good! He is concerned about all the things he has made, and that includes you. He is always checking to make sure you are taken care of. Thank him for his goodness today!

Dear God, thank you for caring so much for me. You are so good.

99

God Has Perfect Timing

God certainly does everything at just the right time.

ECCLESIASTES 3:11 ICB

Do you worry about being late or not having enough time to get things done? Do you hate waiting and need more patience? God always does the right thing at the right time. You can trust him.

Thank you, God, for doing everything at just the right time.

100

God Gives You Rest

"Come to me, all you who are tired and carrying heavy loads. I will give you rest."

MATTHEW 11:28 NIRV

When you feel tired, you can go to God. Sometimes your mind and body feel heavy because there is too much going on. When that happens, you can take everything to God and leave it with him. He will give you rest.

Thank you, God, for taking my heavy loads and giving me rest.